Emojigraphy The International Emoji Language Basic

Emojigraphy The International Emoji Language,
Volume 1

Emojigraphy Team

Published by Emojigraphy.com, 2018

Copyright

EMOJIGRAPHY THE INTERNATIONAL
EMOJI LANGUAGE BASIC
First Edition. July 23, 2018.
Copyright © 2018 Emojigraphy Team.
All Rights Reserved.
ISBN 978-1-5272-2589-3

No part of this publication may be reproduced, stored in a retrieval system or transmitted, in any form or by any means — electronic, mechanical, photocopying, recording or otherwise— without prior written permission from author except for the inclusion of brief quotation embodied in critical reviews.

For information about other books and electronic media, contact the publisher:
Emojigraphy.com
http://emojigraphy.com

The author and publisher shall not be held liable to any person or entity with respect to any loss or damage caused or alleged to be caused directly or indirectly by the information contained within this work. Furthermore, no part of this material may be reprinted or resold.

To **God**, and Our Families,
Thank You With All Our Hearts

Table of Contents

Introduction	1
The Advantages	3
The Concept	6
The Three Tenses and Two Aspects	8
The Grammar	10
Present Tense	16
Past Tense	19
Future Tense	22
In Progress Aspect	25
Completed Aspect	28
Still In Progress (Completed In Progress) Aspect	31
Past Action In Progress	34
Past Action Completed	37
Past Action Still In Progress (Completed In Progress)	40
Future Action In Progress	43
Future Action Completed	47
Future Action Still In Progress(Completed In Progress)	50
Future in the Past (Conditional)	53
Future Action in the Past In Progress	56
Future Action in the Past Completed (Conditional)	59
Future Action in the Past Still In Progress (Completed In Progress)	62
Definite Future Scheduled Routine	66
Definite Future Scheduled Action In Progress	69
Definite Future Unscheduled Action In Progress	72
Definite Future Action Completed	75
Definite Future Action Still In Progress (Completed In Progress)	78
Grammar Comparison	81
Acknowledgement	85
About the Publisher	86

Introduction

Emojigraphy first started as a project to create a useful but easy language for emoji characters. Most of us have used emojis in our online communication but only as an expression of our written text. It gives us a chance to convey the emotion or mood or feeling in our sentences. So we usually add emoji characters before or after our sentences to indicate our emotion towards those sentences.

Then, somehow, more emojis have been created, including not only emotion but regular objects, actions, topics like food, transport, activities, etc. As emoji characters for every topic become more and more available, we are starting to realize that we can use more and more emojis. We have started to use them to replace text words, and the arrangement of emojis has a meaning. Thus, finally, we can use them to create our sentences.

The problem is there is no definitive meaning to these groups of emojis. What we have written can have a different meaning for someone else. But there is a problem when we use emoji characters to create something they were not intended for. An emoji is only a character and it doesn't have proper grammar, which is required to form a consistent meaning. As a result, most sentences created using only emoji characters have different interpretations among different people.

Emojigraphy tries to solve that problem by introducing grammar for emojis. We know it's not easy to design something for people who have different backgrounds in terms of native language and grammar, so because people from all over the world will be using this grammar, we have designed it to be easy to understand and so that it can be used by people of all ages. With this grammar, emoji language is now real. And as we add more features to the language it will become more and more useful and could even become an international language.

> With a humble beginning, we began to think of how we could communicate more consistently using emojis. It needed something—a system to arrange these emojis in a proper pattern. Once we were able to describe the grammar, we knew we would make it, then Emojigraphy was born.
>
> *- The Emojigraphy Team*

The Advantages

International Language

Emojigraphy is the first emoji language intended to be used by people with different native languages. It is the web's lingua franca of visual communication using emojis in the modern age. As a logo- or picture-based (ideograph) written language, we write and read using Emojigraphy. Then we speak Emojigraphy using our mother language.

Universal Language

A picture is what every being sees with their eyes. Emoji language is intuitive. It's understandable and doesn't take a long time to learn, which is why people from all over the world can easily learn it.

Language at the Speed of Sight

You can understand an emoji sentence instantly. There's no need to do much processing in your brain.

Communication Style

Communication is based on positive words. Positive emojis will be used when we create a sentence.

Emoji Grammar

It uses grammar or tenses in sentences, which is compatible with English grammar.

Usability

It is readable and understandable by people with different languages: English, Chinese, Spanish, etc.

Pronunciation

It's spoken in our current language. There are no changes to how we speak.

Writing Style

It has a flexible writing style. Emoji can be used for online writing.

Kanmoji can be used for handwriting.

Suumoji can be used for the number system.

Function

Dual function - as an emoji language and to support the English language.

Usage in Medical Fields

As a therapy tool for stroke patients.

Usage in Education

As a learning tool for early childhood language.

Saves Energy

It saves brain processing power and translation resources. It will save money and natural resources in the end.

> "36% of millennials ages 18 to 34 who use 'visual expressions' such as emojis, GIFs and stickers say that those images better communicate their thoughts and feelings than words do."
> *~Tenor Survey*

> "By 2021, 53.7% of the population will use the internet, equating to 4.14 billion people."
> *~eMarketer Report*

Using Emojigraphy, one might be able to communicate with 4.14 billion people AT ONCE.

The Concept

In Emojigraphy, the emoji language is structured using grammar or tenses. And because Emojigraphy is intended to be used as an international language, we have introduced a concept similar to English tenses, as English is already recognized as an international language.

This choice has a significant advantage for emoji language itself:

1. Emojigraphy can be translated into English with great accuracy (more than 90% accuracy, we hope).
2. English can be translated into Emojigraphy with great accuracy (more than 90% accuracy, we hope).
3. Once translated into English, Emojigraphy can be translated into other languages via regular the translation system of English into other languages.
4. The English language itself has many similarities in grammar to other languages such as Spanish, Portuguese, French, Italian, etc. This will mean Emojigraphy shares the same compatibility with those similar languages.
5. Those who understand English and similar languages will understand Emojigraphy quite easily.
6. Emojigraphy can be used as a tool for beginners to learn English.

Besides other advantages, Emojigraphy itself can be translated directly into other non-English languages.

Throughout this book, we will see some uses of Kanmoji. Kanmoji is the simplified or handwritten version of an emoji with a concept similar to kanji (Chinese or Japanese writing system). For a further introduction to Kanmoji, you can go to :

Kanmoji.com.

In this basic book, we will only describe grammar or tenses of Emojigraphy. Other features of the language such as pronouns, passive sentences, conditionals, questions, and answers will be added in the future in our next book.

The Three Tenses and Two Aspects

In Emojigraphy, we have three tenses and two aspects.

- The tenses relate to the time of speech or event: past, present, future.
- The aspects are concerned with the completion of the action: completed or in progress.

The combination of these tenses and aspects in Emojigraphy is compatible with the 12 main tenses and 9 special tenses of the English language.

In English, tenses are the grammatical forms of verbs, denoting the time of the action or event and the degree of completion. Each tense in the English language has an indication of this grammatical form of the verb by modifying some of the verbs according to time and/or completion. This is similar to Emojigraphy, and we separate them as tenses and aspects on purpose.

In English, the verb sometimes changes according to the tense; in Emojigraphy, the verb never changes because all the words in Emojigraphy are images, which are emoji characters. The emoji for the verb is consistent in sentences regardless of what tenses or aspects are used.

For these tenses and aspects, we give different indications for each of them so we know the grammar without modifying any emojis (images).

When we construct sentences, we must ask ourselves:

1. When does this event or action happen?
Then we must give indication for tenses.

2. What status/stage of completion is the event or action currently in?
Then we must give indication for aspects.

We can't ask in reverse order because we need to know the tenses before we give indication for aspects.

By answering those two questions, we can create Emojigraphy sentences that are compatible with the 12 English language tenses and 9 special tenses.

The next chapters will describe three tenses and the two aspects. Then we will describe the combination of these tenses and aspects.

The Grammar

In Emojigraphy, we have two kinds of grammar:

1. Simplified grammar, indicated as (} at the beginning of an article or document.
2. Full grammar, indicated as (*} at the beginning of an article or document.

Hint: the indication looks like a man facing right.

Simplified Grammar

In simplified grammar, we see an event or action as a task. There are 5 stages of a task, and our sentence should be in one of those stages:

1. Planning. An event or action is registered, acknowledged: use future tense.

2. Upcoming. An event or action is in the near future, assigned or ready.
- If it has been prepared: use definite future scheduled action in progress.
- If it hasn't been prepared: use definite future unscheduled action in progress.

3. Doing. An event or action is happening: use in progress aspect.

4. Done. An event or action has happened, become an experience: use completed aspect.

5. History. An event or action was happened, logged or archived: use past tense.

- For sentences that only describe a habit, fact, or generalization: use present tense.

Using simplified grammar is easier for people whose native language has little to no grammar. Therefore, for these people, transitioning from their native language to Emojigraphy will be easier.

Simplified grammar is also a useful way to learn Emojigraphy step by step. We learn and use simplified grammar first; then, as we gain a greater understanding about grammar combinations, we use full grammar.

The translation from Emojigraphy with simplified grammar into English will also become less accurate because the writer only use 7 tenses combinations so the reader needs to interpret and guess which compatible English tenses should be used for the translation.

Full Grammar

In full grammar, we use the three tenses and two aspects.

Using full grammar is easier for people whose native language incorporates grammar that is similar to English grammar. Therefore, for these people, the transition from their native language to Emojigraphy will be easier.

Although this book explains many tenses, we only have to learn the three tenses and two aspects and use the combination of those five factors to create English compatible tenses in our sentences.

Sentence Structure

All tenses and aspects follow the structure of subject-verb-object (SVO) in a sentence by default. This means that we put the verb after the subject and before the object.

- Subject = who performs the action.
- Verb = action.
- Object = who receives the action.

However, the structure of subject-object-verb (SOV) in a sentence is also acceptable. This is useful for native language people using SOV structure, such as the Japanese and the Koreans.

At the beginning of the sentences or books or documents using Emojigraphy, we need to put the grammar and sentence structure choice of our writing:

- Subject = . (period)
- Verb = ; (semicolon)
- Object = , (comma)

1. The sign (*} means that we use default full grammar, with the SVO structure. An article or document or sentence without any sign will use this setting as default.
2. The sign (*.,;} means that we use full grammar with the SOV structure.
3. The sign (*;..} means that we use full grammar with the VSO structure.
4. The sign (*;,.} means that we use full grammar with the VOS structure.
5. The sign (*,;.} means that we use full grammar with the OVS structure.
6. The sign (*,.;} means that we use full grammar with the OSV structure.
7. The sign (} means that we use simplified grammar with the SVO structure.
8. The sign (.,;} means that we use simplified grammar with the SOV structure.

For right-to-left writing direction, there are no changes in grammar rules and placement of indication characters, but the signs have to be changed:
- The sign {*) means that we use right-to-left writing direction, default full grammar with the SVO structure.
- The sign {;,.*) means that we use right-to-left writing direction, full grammar with the SOV structure.
- The sign {) means that we use right-to-left writing direction, simplified grammar with the SVO structure.
- The sign {;,.) means that we use right-to-left writing direction, simplified grammar with the SOV structure.

Root Words

In learning to construct a sentence, we need to know the concept of root words. A root word is the original form of a word from the dictionary. It is the simple form of the word.

- Root word for had = have
- Root word for made = make
- Root word for paid = pay
- Root word for sent = send
- Root word for gave = give
- Root word for given = give
- Root word for spoke = speak
- Root word for spoken = speak
- Root word for creation = create
- Root word for creative = create
- Root word for creatively = create
- Root word for creativity = create

Example original sentence:

I will have been <u>working</u> for two hours by the time you arrive.

Example root word:

I <u>work</u> for two hours by the time you arrive.

In Emojigraphy, we only use root words to create a sentence. Root words are meant to differentiate between grammar and words in Emojigraphy. By separating grammar and words, we can only focus on words when reading Emojigraphy documents without paying attention to grammar. This has advantages. You can skim over the document quickly to know the topic of that document, as the topic of the document has nothing to do with grammar. In the example above, we know the topic of the document is about working when someone comes.

Present Tense

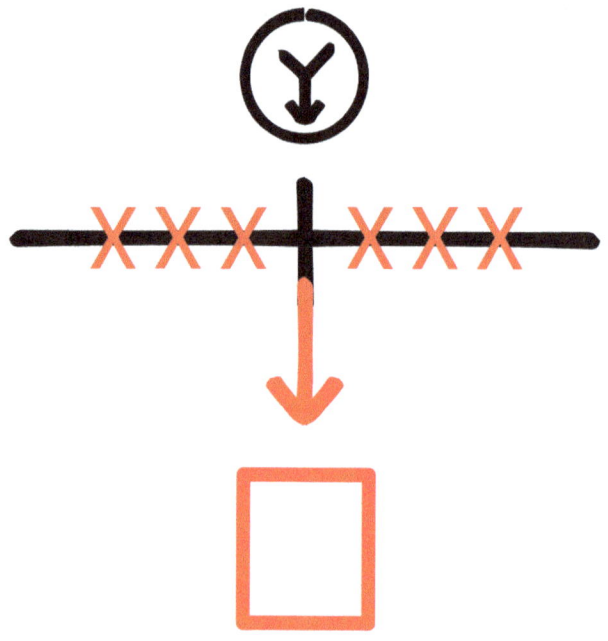

Present tense represents an event as taking place or a state existing in present time, usually to show repetition, habits, facts or generalization.

Compatible English Tense: Simple Present Tense.

English Tense Verb Form: Verb.

Indication Character: (none).

Location of Indication Character: On the Root Word Verb.

Usage: Root Word

Emoji:

Kanmoji:

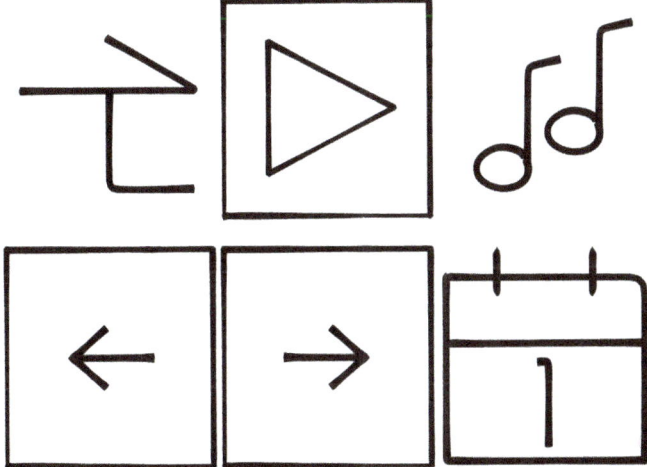

Root Words: (I) (play) (music) (left arrow + right arrow + tearoff calendar = every day).

English Translation: I play music every day.

Past Tense

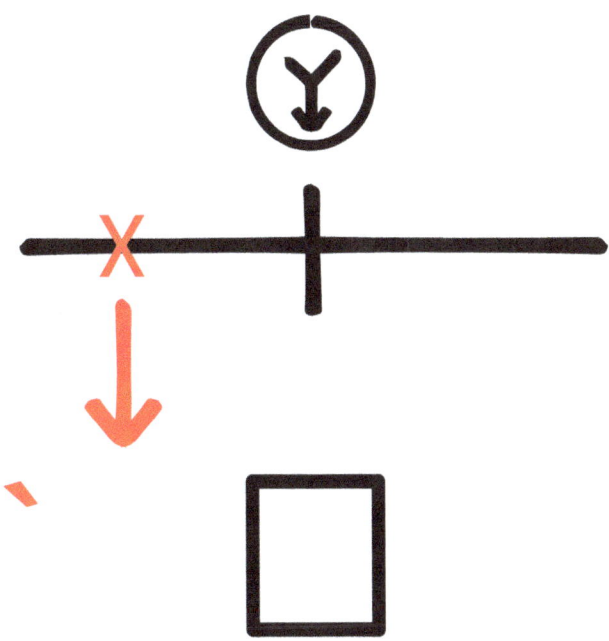

Past tense represents an event or state that took place at a specific time in the past, usually to talk about past habits, facts or generalization.

Compatible English Tense: Simple Past Tense.

English Tense Verb Form: Past Tense Verb.

Indication Character: ` (grave accent).

Location of Indication Character: On the (farthest) Left Side of the Root Word Verb.

Usage: `Root Word

Tip: You can increase the font size of indication character to increase visibility.

Emoji:

Kanmoji:

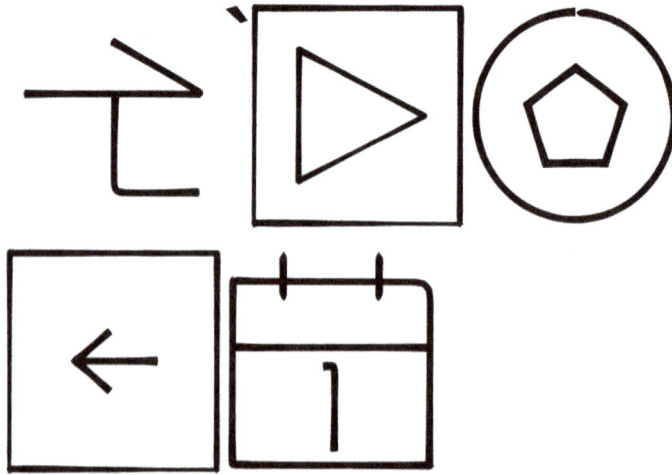

Root Words: (I) `(play) (football) (left arrow + tearoff calendar = yesterday).

English Translation: I played football yesterday.

Future Tense

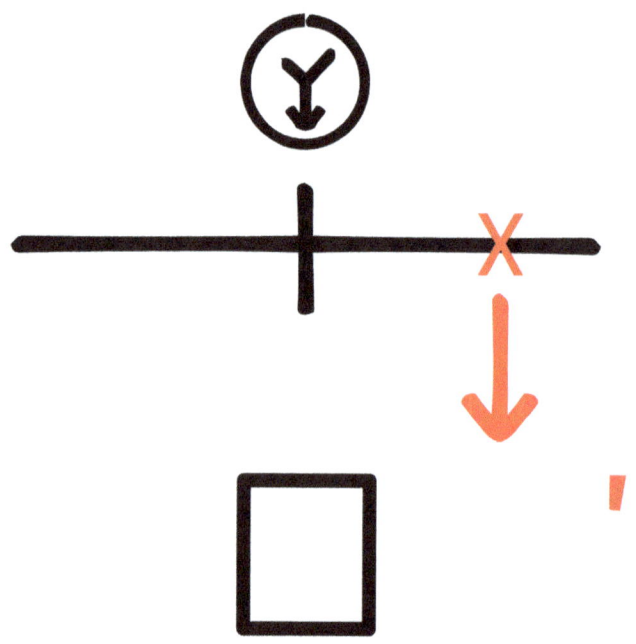

Future tense represents an event, state or fact that would or will take place or exist in the future time.

Compatible English Tense: Simple Future Tense.

English Tense Verb Form: Shall/Will + Verb.

Indication Character: ' (apostrophe).

Location of Indication Character: On the Right Side of the Root Word Verb.

EMOJIGRAPHY THE INTERNATIONAL EMOJI LANGUAGE BASIC   23

Usage: Root Word'

The right side of the root word verb is intended as the place for future events or actions.

Tip: You can increase the font size of indication character to increase visibility.

Emoji:

Kanmoji:

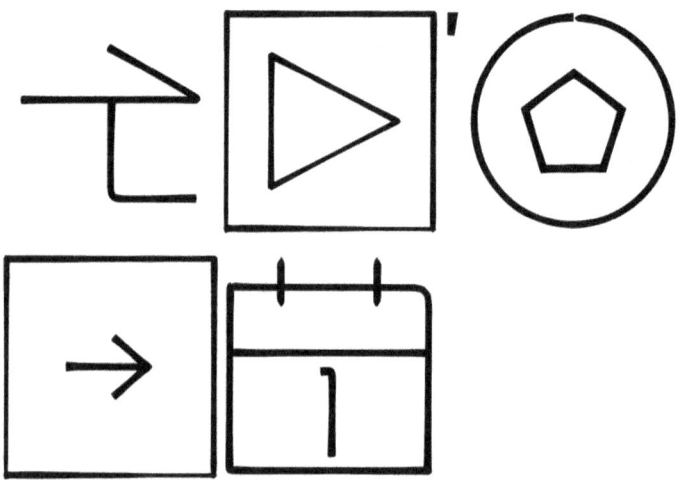

Root Words: (I) (play)' (football) (right arrow + tearoff calendar = tomorrow).

English Translation: I will play football tomorrow.

In Progress Aspect

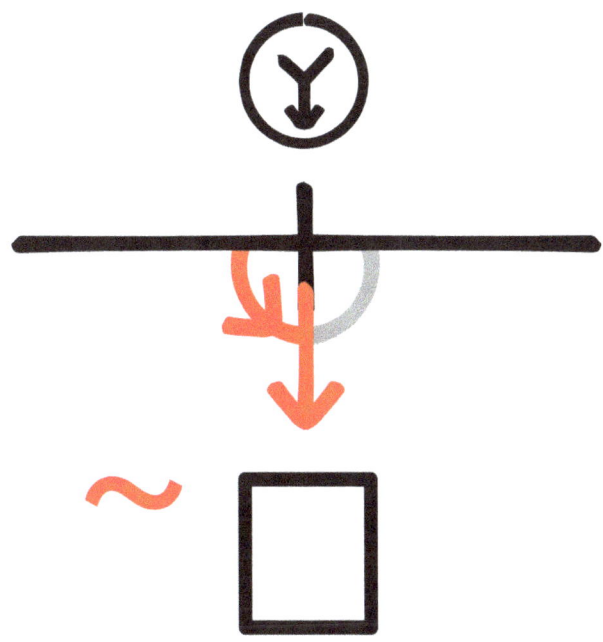

The in progress aspect represents an action or event that is in progress state and continues for a period.

Compatible English Tense: Present Continuous Tense.

English Tense Verb Form: am/is/are + Verb + ing.

Indication Character: ~ (tilde).

Location of Indication Character: Next to the Left Side of the Root Word Verb.

Usage: ~Root Word

Emoji:

Kanmoji:

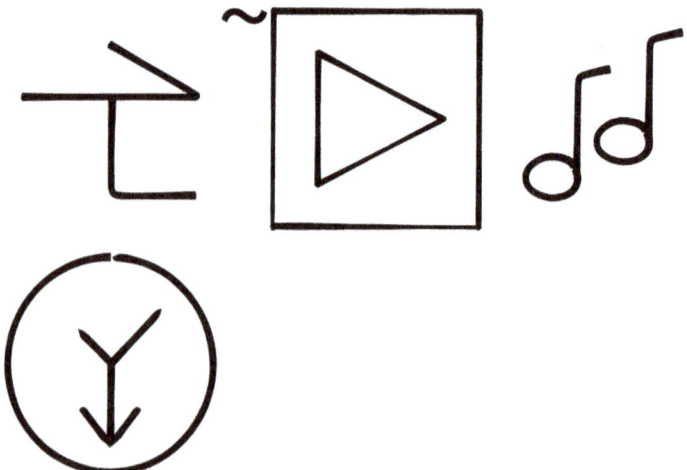

Root Words: (I) ~(play) (music) (now).

English Translation: I am playing music now.

Completed Aspect

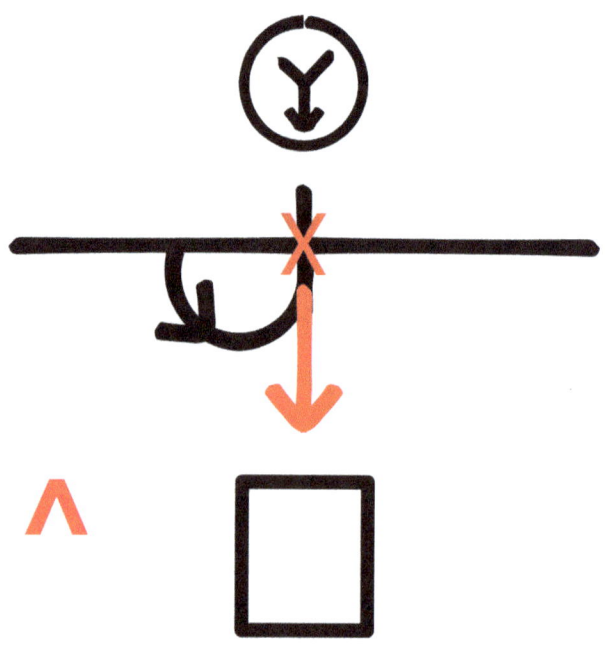

The completed aspect represents an action or event that has already begun and is in a completed state by a particular point in time.

Compatible English Tense: Present Perfect Tense.

English Tense Verb Form: Have/Has + Past Participle.

Indication Character: ^ (circumflex accent).

Location of Indication Character: On the Left Side of the

Root Word Verb.

Usage: ^Root Word

Emoji:

Kanmoji:

Root Words: (I) ^(sleep) (down arrow + right arrow + three o'clock = since three o'clock).

English Translation: I have slept since three o'clock.

Still In Progress (Completed In Progress) Aspect

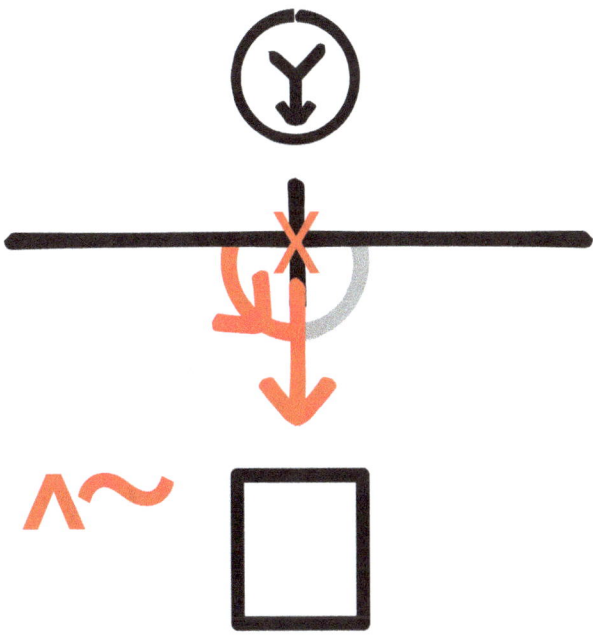

The still in progress aspect represents an action or event that has already begun and is still in progress state and continues for a period.

Compatible English Tense: Present Perfect Continuous Tense.

English Tense Verb Form: Have/Has Been + Verb + ing.

Indication Character: ^~ (circumflex accent + tilde).

Location of Indication Character: Next to the Left Side of

the Root Word Verb.

Usage: ^~Root Word

Emoji:

EMOJIGRAPHY THE INTERNATIONAL EMOJI LANGUAGE BASIC

Kanmoji:

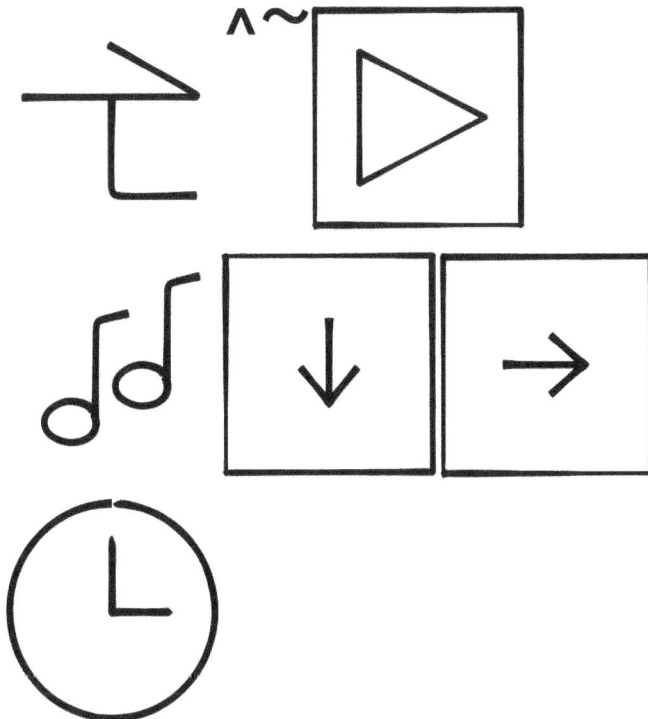

Root Words: (I) ^~(play) (music) (down arrow + right arrow + three o'clock = since three o'clock).

English Translation: I have been playing music since three o'clock.

Past Action In Progress

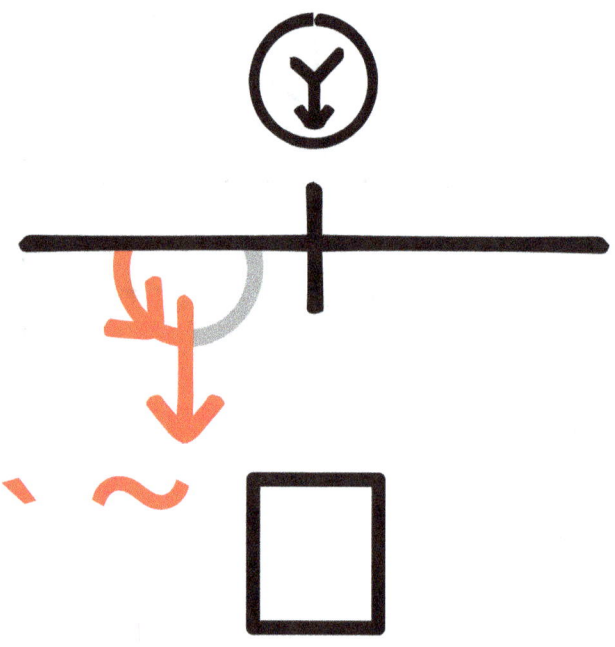

Past action in progress represents an action or event in the past but which is still in progress state and not yet completed.

Compatible English Tense: Past Continuous Tense.

English Tense Verb Form: Was/Were + Verb + ing.

Indication Character: ` ~ (grave accent + tilde).

Location of Indication Character: On the (farthest) Left Side of the Root Word Verb.

EMOJIGRAPHY THE INTERNATIONAL EMOJI LANGUAGE BASIC

Usage: ` ~Root Word

Emoji:

Kanmoji:

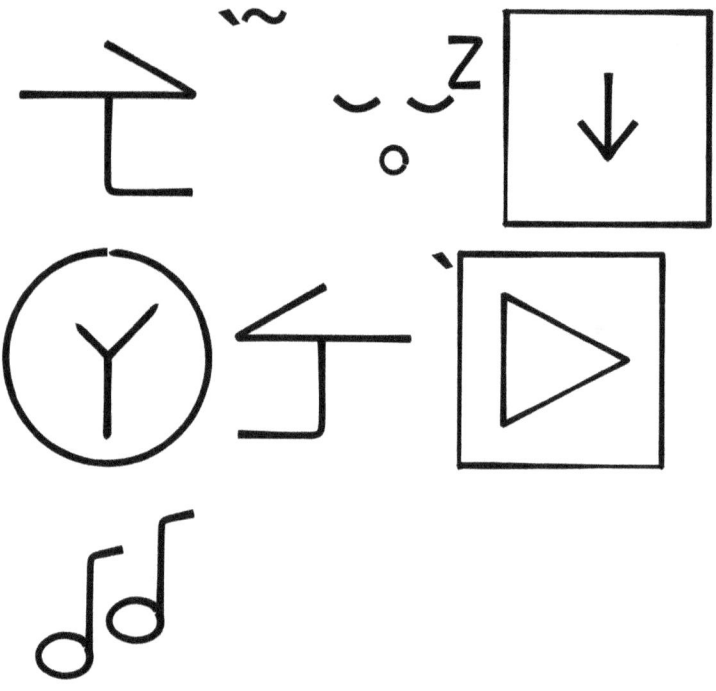

Root Words: (I) `~(sleep) (down arrow + time = when) (you) `(play) (music).

English Translation: I was sleeping when you played music.

Past Action Completed

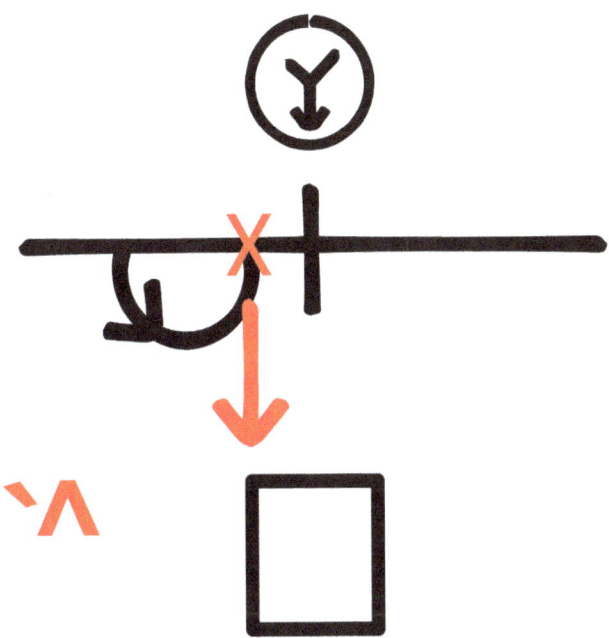

Past action completed represents an action or event that has already begun and is in a completed state in the past.

Compatible English Tense: Past Perfect Tense.

English Tense Verb Form: Had + Past Participle.

Indication Character: `^ (grave accent + circumflex accent).

Location of Indication Character: On the (farthest) Left Side of the Root Word Verb.

Usage: `^Root Word

Emoji:

Kanmoji:

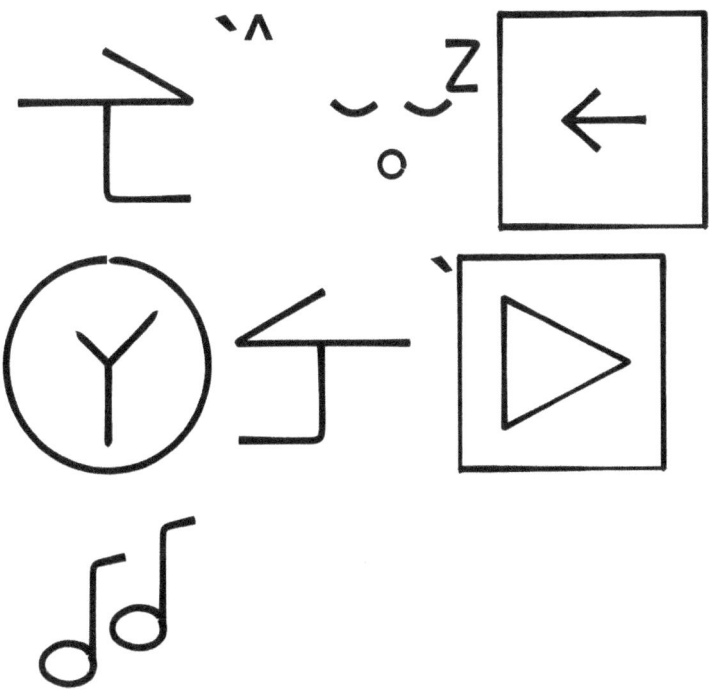

Root Words: (I) `^(sleep) (left arrow + time = before) (you) `(play) (music).

English Translation: I had slept before you played music.

Past Action Still In Progress (Completed In Progress)

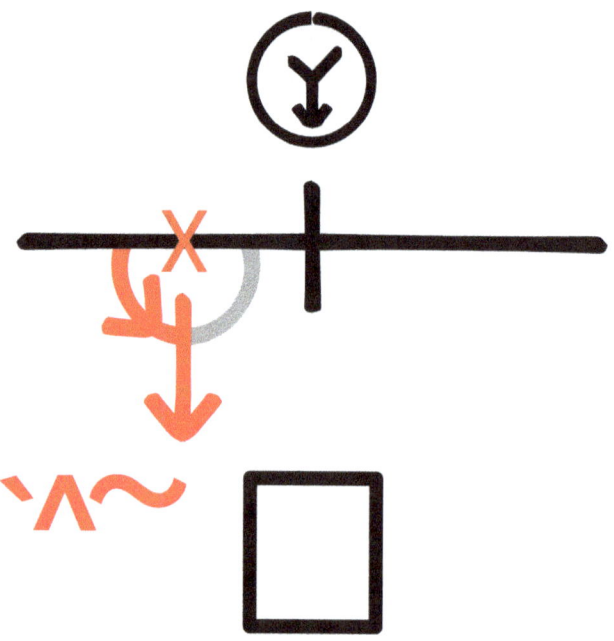

Past action still in progress represents an action or event that began before the given moment in the past, and continued up to that time or stopped just before it.

Compatible English Tense: Past Perfect Continuous Tense.

English Tense Verb Form: Had Been + Verb + ing.

Indication Character: `^~ (grave accent + circumflex accent + tilde).

Location of Indication Character: On the (farthest) Left Side of the Root Word Verb.

Usage: `^~Root Word

Emoji:

Kanmoji:

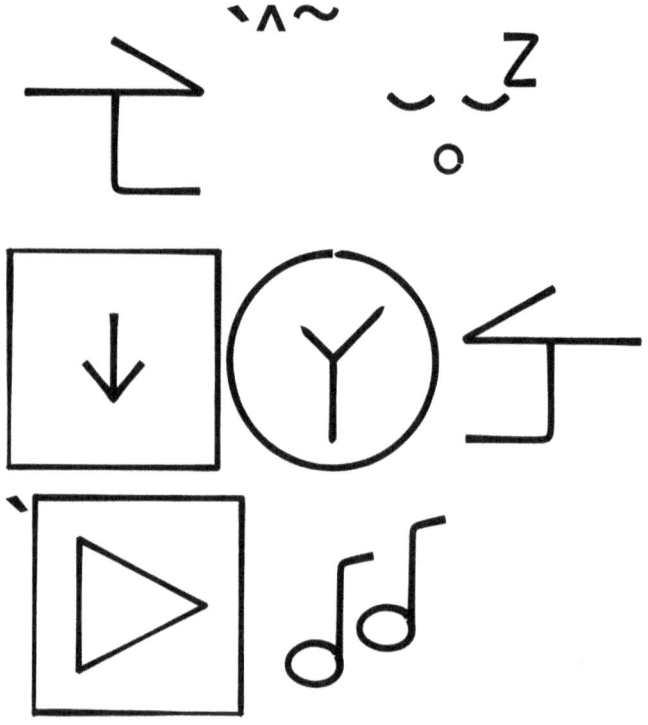

Root Words: (I) `^~(sleep) (down arrow + time = when) (you) `(play) (music).

English Translation: I had been sleeping when you played music.

Future Action In Progress

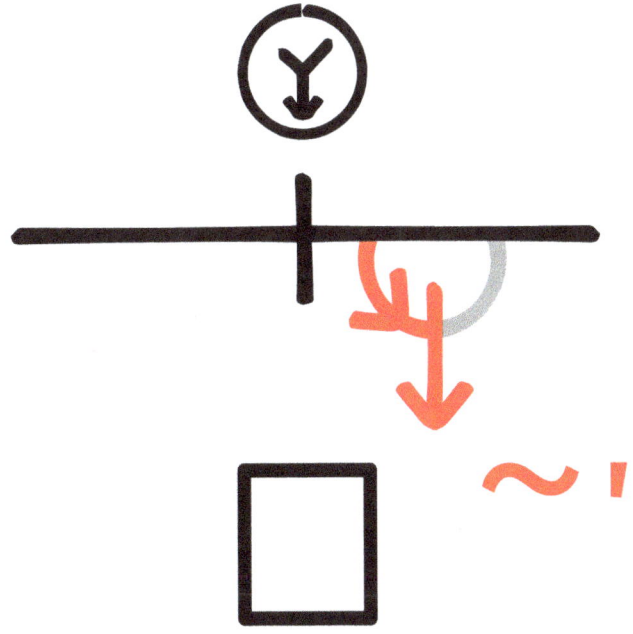

Future action in progress represents an action or event in the future but which is still in progress state and not yet completed.

Compatible English Tense: Future Continuous Tense.

English Tense Verb Form: Shall/Will Be + Verb + ing.

Indication Character: ~' (tilde + apostrophe).

Location of Indication Character: On the Right Side of the

Root Word Verb, Apostrophe is on the (farthest) Right Side of the Root Word Verb.

Usage: Root Word~'

The Character ~ (tilde) indicates an in progress aspect, which means that an action is in the process of happening and continues to do so. Normally it is placed on the left of the root word verb, right next to the root word verb.

In this tense, the tilde is moved to the right of the root word verb, the area of the future events or actions, but still on the left of the future tense indicator (apostrophe), which means that this future tense has the in progress aspect of the tilde —it will become an in progress aspect when happening in the future.

EMOJIGRAPHY THE INTERNATIONAL EMOJI LANGUAGE BASIC   **45**

Emoji:

Kanmoji:

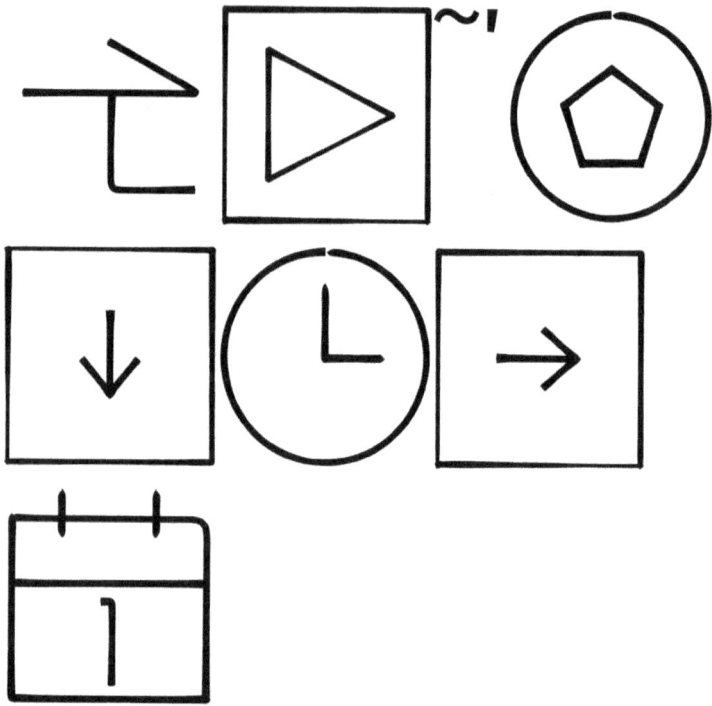

Root Words: (I) (play)~' (football) (at) (three o'clock) (right arrow + tear off calendar = tomorrow).

English Translation: I will be playing football at three o'clock tomorrow.

Future Action Completed

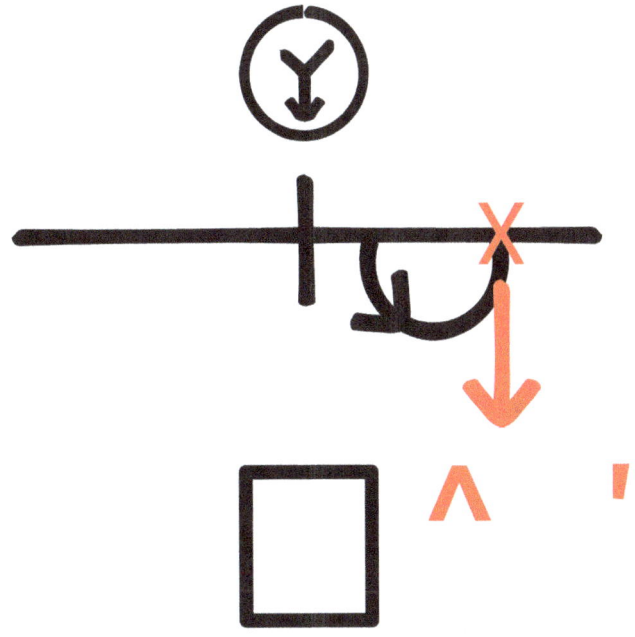

Future action completed represents an action or event that has already begun and will be in a completed state at a future time.

Compatible English Tense: Future Perfect Tense.

English Tense Verb Form: Shall/Will Have + Past Participle.

Indication Character: ^' (circumflex accent + apostrophe).

Location of Indication Character: On the Right Side of the

Root Word Verb, Apostrophe is on the (farthest) Right Side of the Root Word Verb.

Usage: Root Word^'

Emoji:

EMOJIGRAPHY THE INTERNATIONAL EMOJI LANGUAGE BASIC 49

Kanmoji:

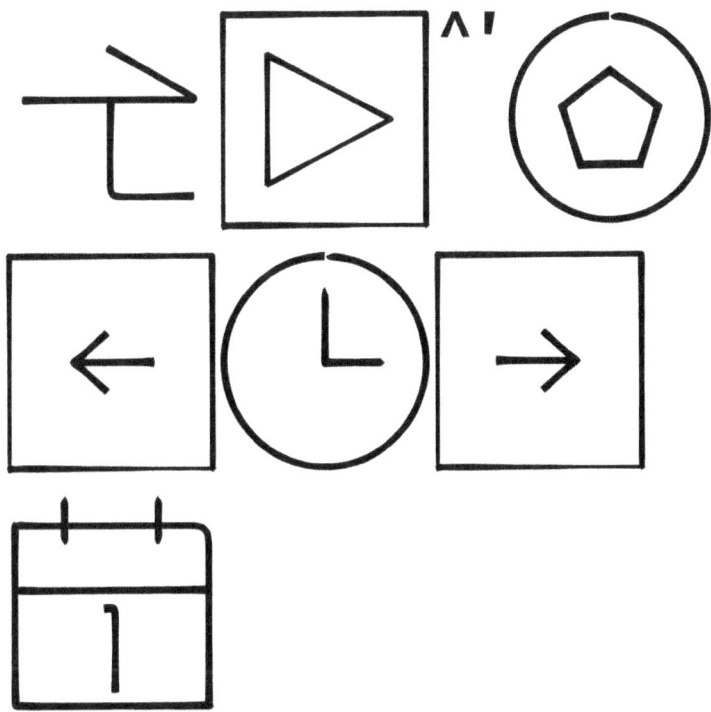

Root Words: (I) (play)^' (football) (before) (three o'clock) (right arrow + tear off calendar = tomorrow).

English Translation: I will have played football before three o'clock tomorrow.

Future Action Still In Progress
(Completed In Progress)

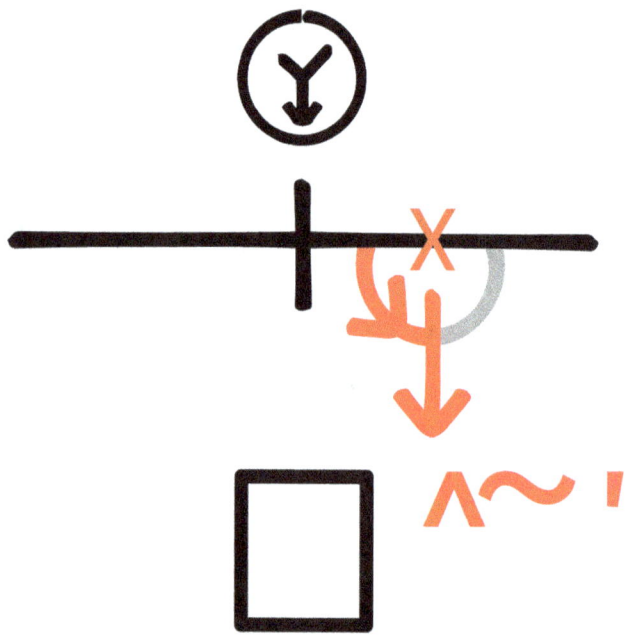

Future action still in progress represents an action or event that begins before the given moment of future time and continues up to that time.

Compatible English Tense: Future Perfect Continuous Tense.

English Tense Verb Form: Shall/Will Have Been + Verb + ing.

Indication Character: ^~' (circumflex accent + tilde + apostrophe).

EMOJIGRAPHY THE INTERNATIONAL EMOJI LANGUAGE BASIC 51

Location of Indication Character: On the Right Side of the Root Word Verb, Apostrophe is on the (farthest) Right Side of the Root Word Verb.

Usage: Root Word^~'

Emoji:

Kanmoji:

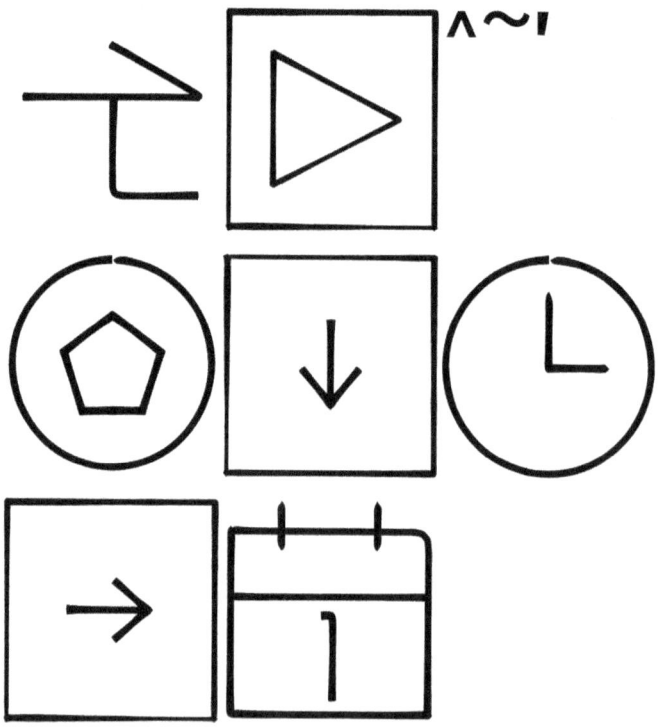

Root Words: (I) (play)^~' (football) (at) (three o'clock) (right arrow + tear off calendar = tomorrow).

English Translation: I will have been playing football at three o'clock tomorrow.

Future in the Past (Conditional)

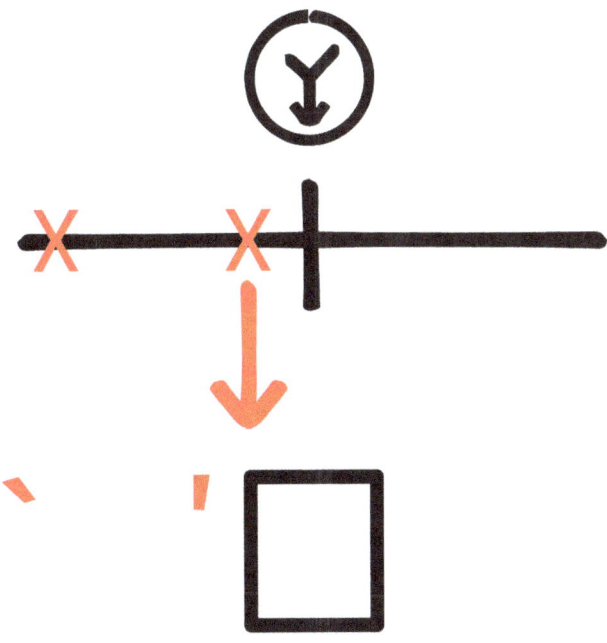

Future in the past is the past form of the future tense that represents an event or state that took place in a past time, such as past habits.

Compatible English Tense: Past Future Tense.

English Tense Verb Form: Should/Would + Verb.

Indication Character: ` and ' (grave accent and apostrophe).

Location of Indication Character: Grave Accent is on the (farthest) Left Side of the Root Word Verb, Apostrophe is Next on the Left Side of the Root Word Verb.

Usage: `'Root Word

Emoji:

Kanmoji:

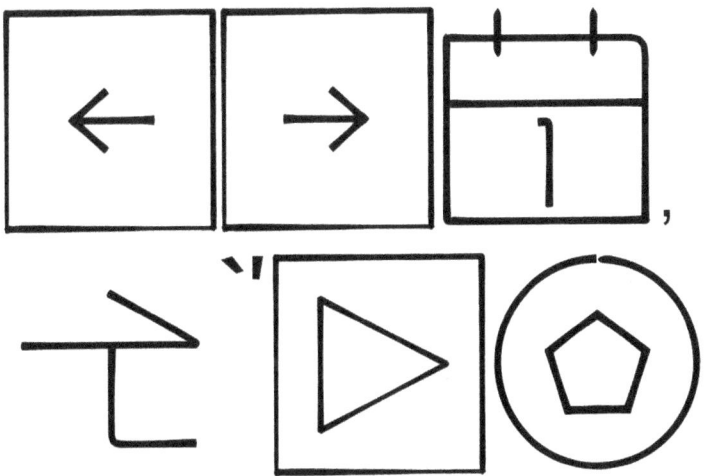

Root Words: (left arrow + right arrow + tear off calendar = every day), (I) `'(play) (football).

English Translation: Every day, I should play football.

Future Action in the Past In Progress

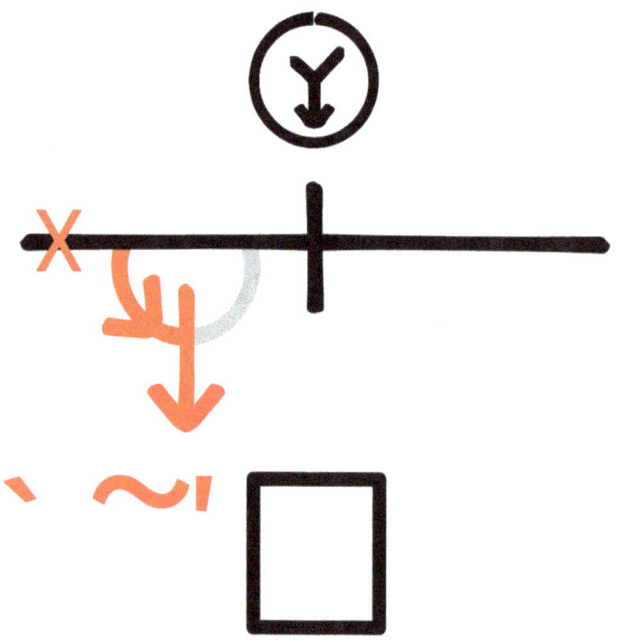

Future action in the past in progress is the past form of the future action in progress that represents an action or event that took place in a past time and which is still in progress state and not yet completed.

Compatible English Tense: Past Future Continuous Tense.

English Tense Verb Form: Should/Would Be + Verb + ing.

Indication Character: '~' (grave accent + tilde + apostrophe).

EMOJIGRAPHY THE INTERNATIONAL EMOJI LANGUAGE BASIC 57

Location of Indication Character: On the Left Side of the Root Word Verb, Grave Accent is on the (farthest) Left Side of the Root Word Verb.

Usage: ` ~'Root Word

Emoji:

Kanmoji:

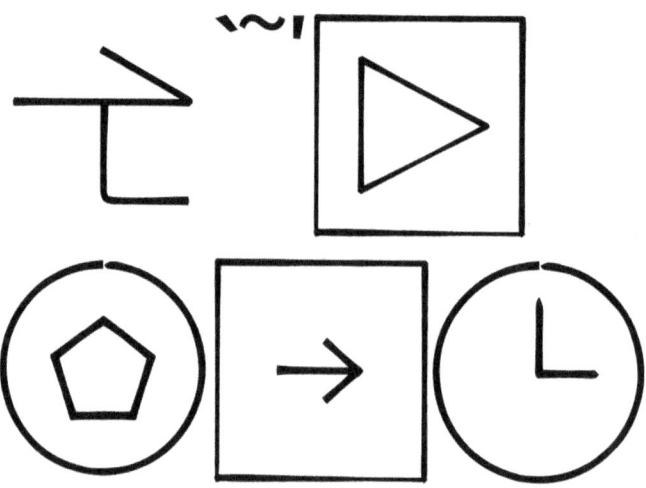

Root Words: (I) ` ~'(play) (football) (after) (three o'clock).

English Translation: I would be playing football after three o'clock.

Future Action in the Past Completed (Conditional)

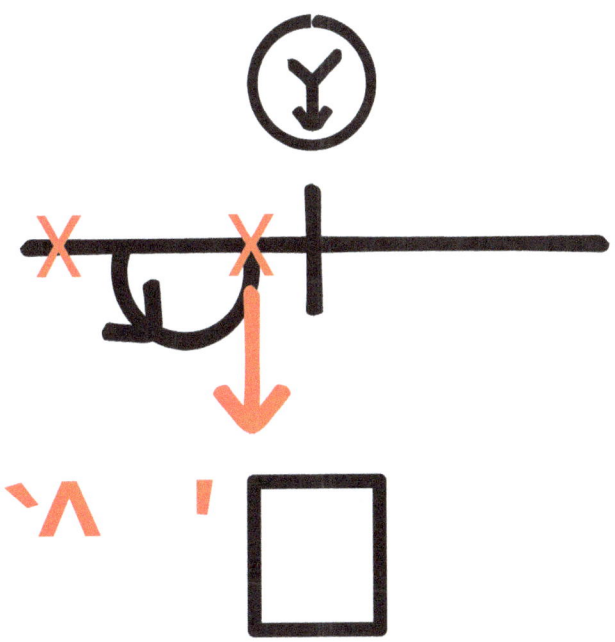

Future action in the past completed is the past form of the future action completed that represents an action or event that took place in a past time that has already begun and is in a completed state.

Compatible English Tense: Past Future Perfect Tense.

English Tense Verb Form: Should/Would Have + Past Participle.

Indication Character: '`^'' (grave accent + circumflex accent + apostrophe).

Location of Indication Character: On the Left Side of the Root Word Verb, Grave Accent is on the (farthest) Left Side of the Root Word Verb.

Usage: `^'Root Word

Emoji:

Kanmoji:

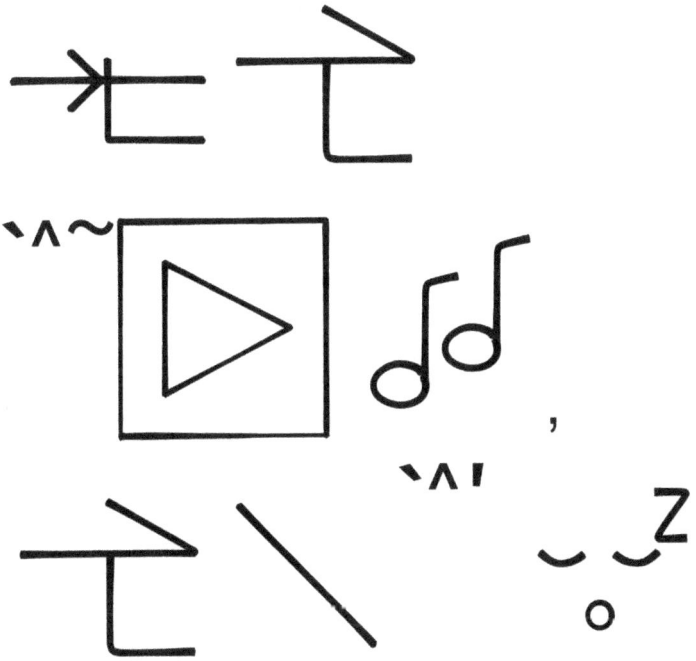

Root Words: (if) (I) `^~(play) (music), (I) (not) `^'(sleep).

English Translation: If I had been playing music, I wouldn't have slept.

Future Action in the Past Still In Progress (Completed In Progress)

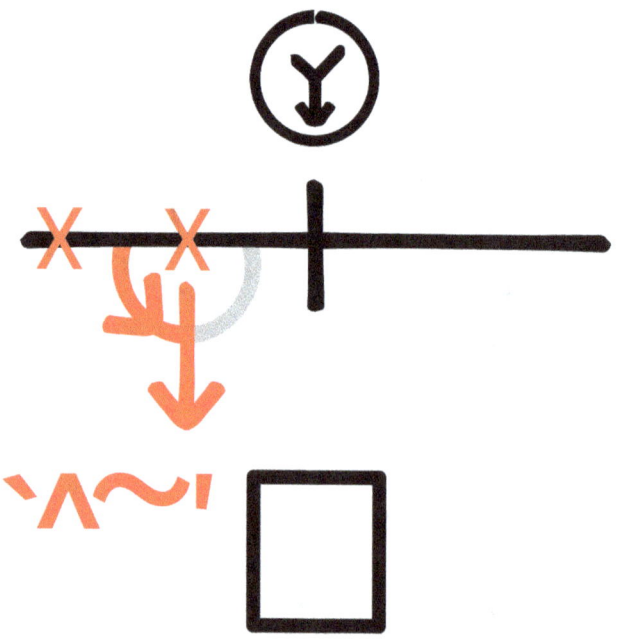

Future action in the past still in progress is the past form of the future action still in progress, which represents an action or event that took place in a past time that has already begun, is still in progress state and not yet completed.

Compatible English Tense: Past Future Perfect Continuous Tense.

English Tense Verb Form: Should/Would Have Been + Past Participle + ing.

EMOJIGRAPHY THE INTERNATIONAL EMOJI LANGUAGE BASIC 63

Indication Character: `^~' (grave accent + circumflex accent + tilde + apostrophe).

Location of Indication Character: On the Left Side of the Root Word Verb, Grave Accent is on the (farthest) Left Side of the Root Word Verb.

Usage: `^~'Root Word

Emoji:

Kanmoji:

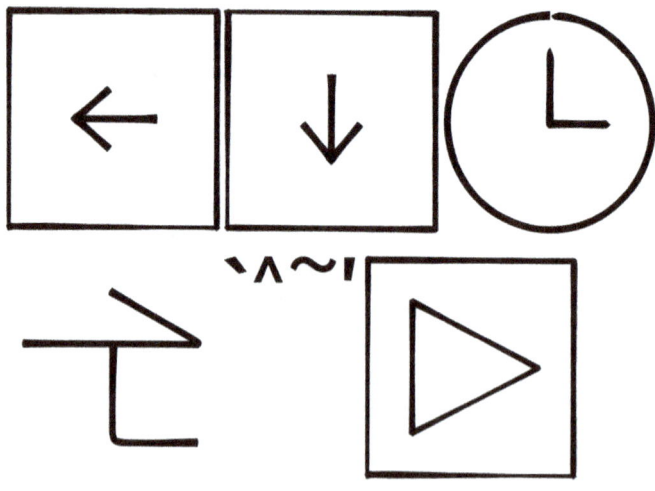

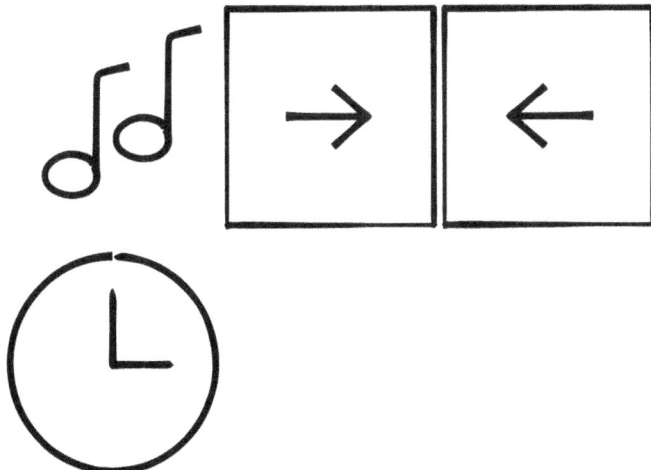

Root Words: (left arrow + down arrow + three o'clock = by three o'clock) (I) `^~'(play) (music) (right arrow + left arrow + three o'clock = for three hours).

English Translation: By three o'clock I would have been playing music for three hours.

Definite Future Scheduled Routine

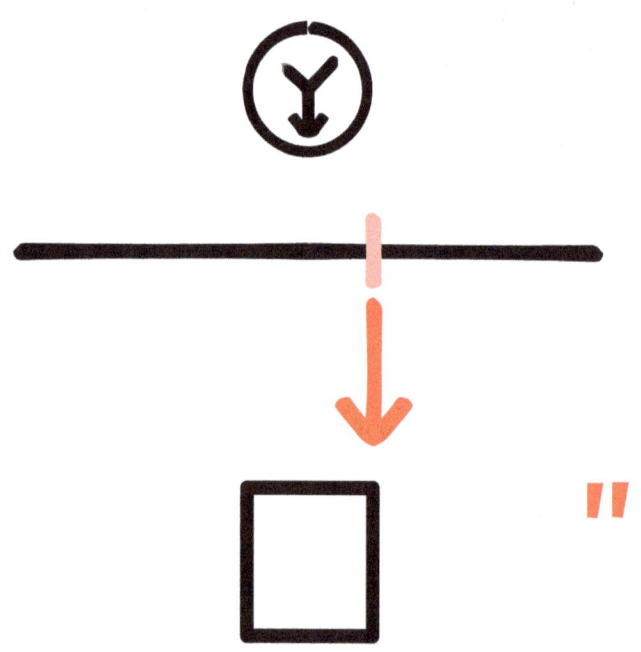

A definite future scheduled routine represents an event or fact that will likely happen. In the future, this event or fact will definitively change to become present tense because it is a scheduled routine.

Compatible English Tense: Simple Present Tense for Future Scheduled Events.

English Tense Verb Form: Verb.

Indication Character: ' and ' (apostrophe and apostrophe).

Location of Indication Character: Next to the Right Side of the Root Word Verb, Apostrophe is on the (farthest) Right Side of the Root Word Verb.

Usage: Root Word"

Remember, the right side of the root word verb is intended as the place for future events or actions.

The second apostrophe indication means that it has a strong probability (almost 100%) of happening.

Emoji:

Kanmoji:

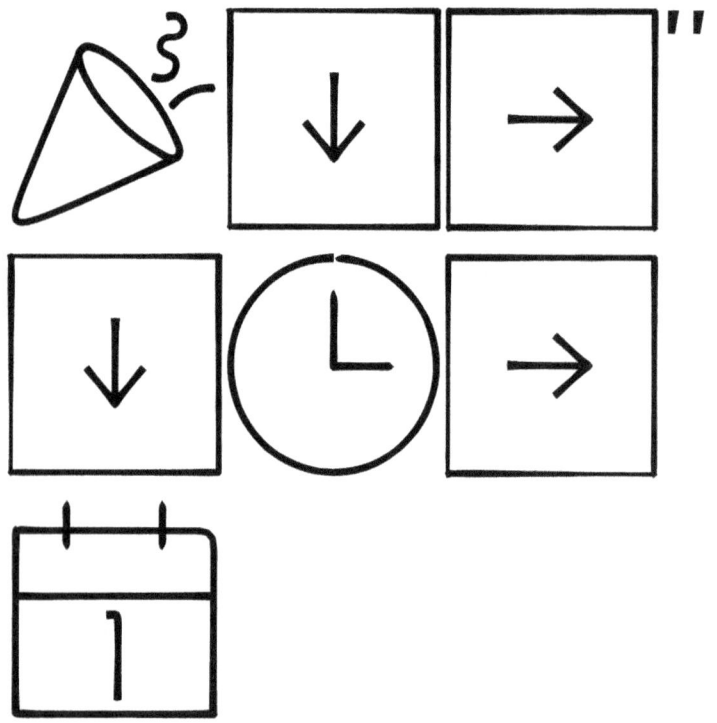

Root Words: (party) (down arrow + right arrow = start)" (down arrow + 3 o'clock = at three o'clock) (right arrow + tearoff calendar = tomorrow).

English Translation: The party starts at 3:00 tomorrow.

Definite Future Scheduled Action In Progress

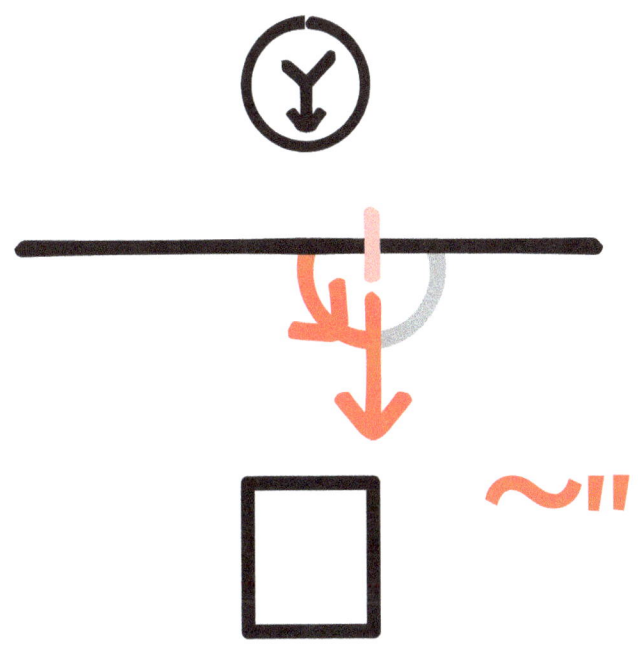

A definite future scheduled action in progress represents an event or fact that will likely happen (almost 100% probability). In the future, this event or fact will definitively change to become an in progress aspect (is happening) because it is a scheduled plan or arrangement.

Compatible English Tense: Present Continuous Tense for Future Arrangements.

English Tense Verb Form: am/is/are + Verb + ing.

Indication Character: ~" (tilde + apostrophe + apostrophe).

Location of Indication Character: Next to the Right Side of the Root Word Verb, Apostrophe is on the (farthest) Right Side of the Root Word Verb.

Usage: Root Word~"

Remember, the right side of the root word verb is intended as the place for future events or actions.

Emoji:

Kanmoji:

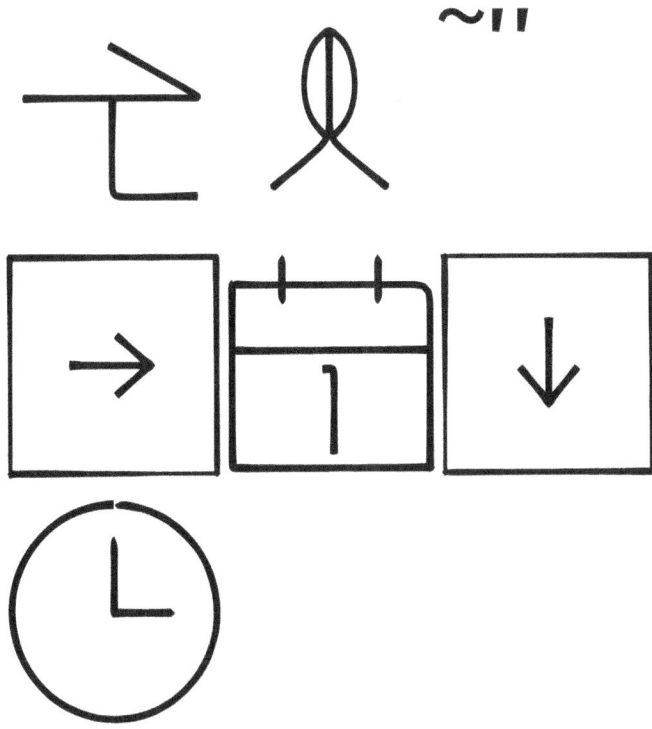

Root Words: (I) (pray)~" (right arrow + tearoff calendar = tomorrow) (down arrow + three o'clock = at three o'clock).

English Translation: I am praying tomorrow at three o'clock.

Definite Future Unscheduled Action In Progress

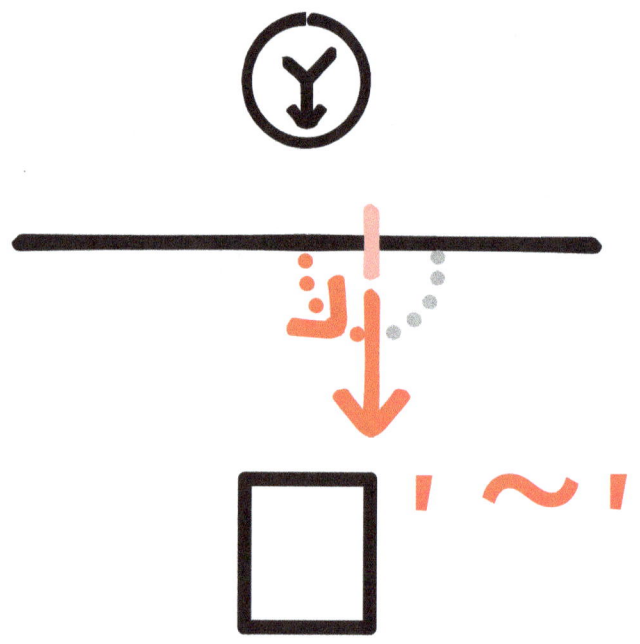

A definite future unscheduled action in progress represents an event or fact that will likely happen (almost 100% probability). In the future, this event or fact will definitively change to become an in progress aspect (is happening) because:

- the subject has an intention to make it happen but has not scheduled/arranged it yet, or

- there is no arrangement needed, such as definite prediction (weather, sickness, etc.), or

- the event or fact refers to the immediate or near future.

Compatible English Tense: Present Continuous Tense for Future Intention/Prediction.

English Tense Verb Form: am/is/are + Going To + Verb.

Indication Character: '~' (apostrophe + tilde + apostrophe).

Location of Indication Character: Next to the Right Side of the Root Word Verb.

Usage: Root Word'~'

Remember, the right side of the root word verb is intended as the place for future events or actions.

The second apostrophe is placed on the left of an aspect, far from the first apostrophe, which means that this definite future action has not been scheduled/arranged yet, there is no arrangement needed or it is in the near future.

Emoji:

Kanmoji:

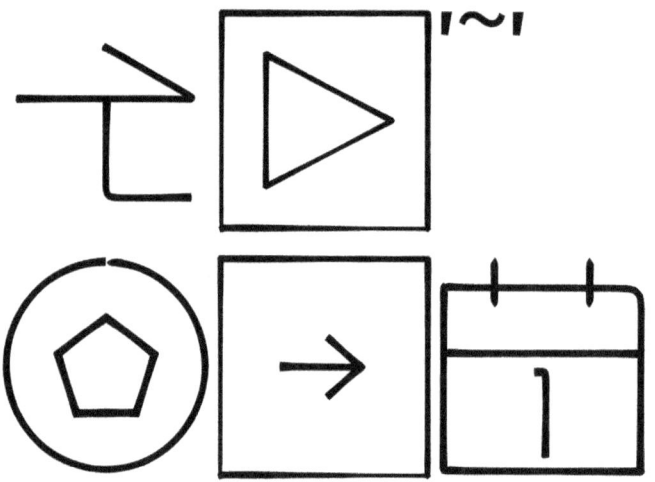

Root Words: (I) (play)'~' (football) (right arrow + tearoff calendar = tomorrow).

English Translation: I am going to play football tomorrow.

Definite Future Action Completed

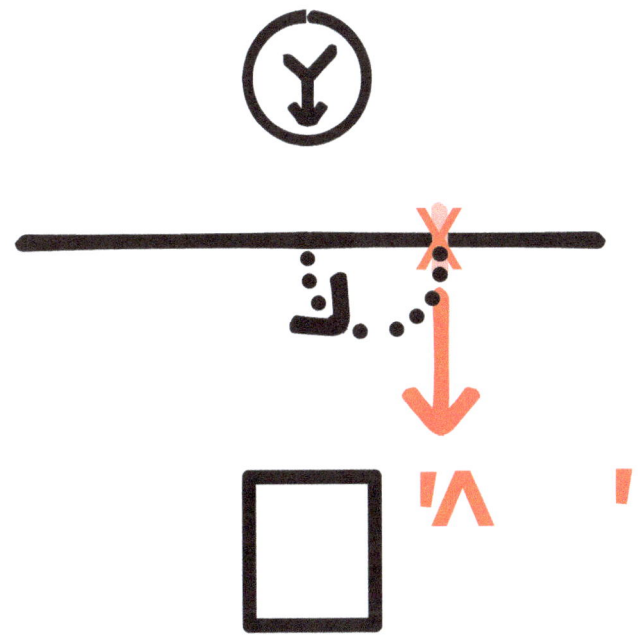

A definite future action completed represents an event or fact that will likely happen (almost 100% probability). In the future, this event or fact will definitively change to become a completed aspect (has happened) because:

- the subject has an intention to make it happen, or

- a definite assumption based on habit.

Compatible English Tense: Future Perfect Tense for Expected Action.

English Tense Verb Form: Shall/Will Have + Past Participle.

Indication Character: ' and ^ and ' (apostrophe and circumflex accent and apostrophe).

Location of Indication Character: Next to the Right Side of the Root Word Verb.

Usage: Root Word'^'

Remember, the right side of the root word verb is intended as the place for future events or actions.

Emoji:

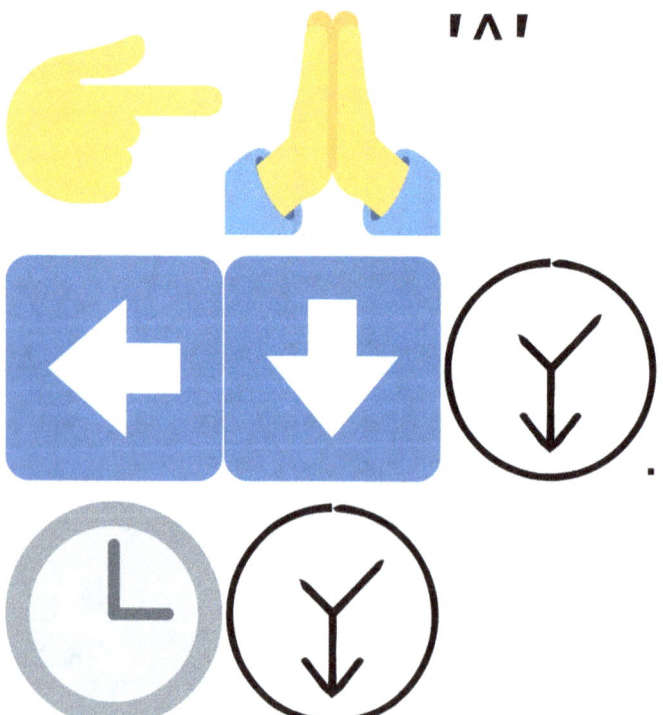

EMOJIGRAPHY THE INTERNATIONAL EMOJI LANGUAGE BASIC 77

Kanmoji:

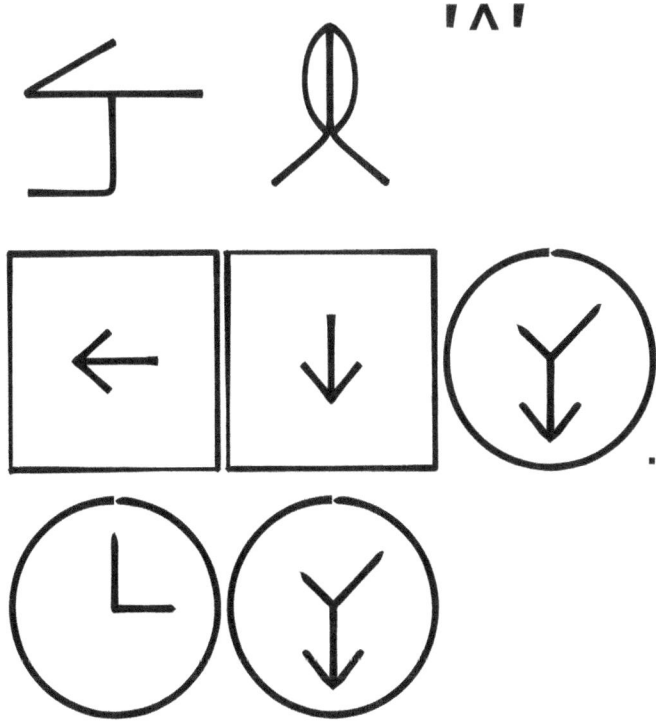

Root Words: (you) (pray)'^' (left arrow + down arrow = by) (now). (three o'clock) (now).

English Translation: You will have prayed by now. It's three o'clock now.

Definite Future Action Still In Progress (Completed In Progress)

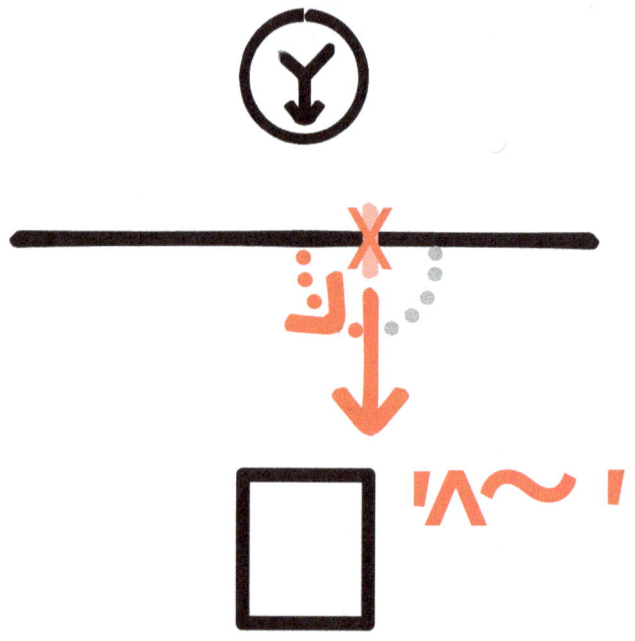

A definite future action still in progress represents an event or fact that will likely happen (almost 100% probability). In the future, this event or fact will definitively change to become a still in progress aspect (has been happening) because:

- the subject has an intention to make it happen, or

- a definite assumption based on habit.

Compatible English Tense: Future Perfect Continuous Tense for Expected Actions.

English Tense Verb Form: Shall/Will Have + Been + ing.

Indication Character: ' and ^~ and ' (apostrophe and circumflex accent + tilde and apostrophe).

Location of Indication Character: Next to the Right Side of the Root Word Verb.

Usage: Root Word'^~'

Remember, the right side of the root word verb is intended as the place for future events or actions.

Emoji:

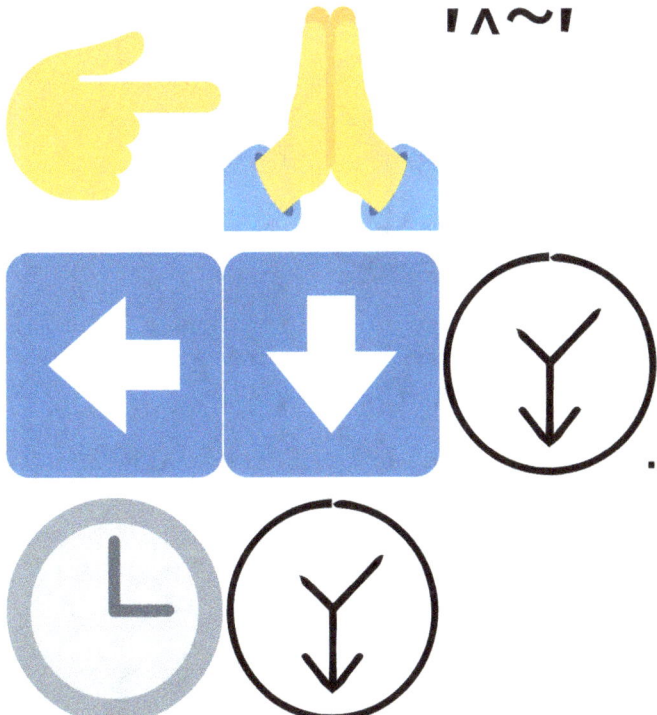

Kanmoji:

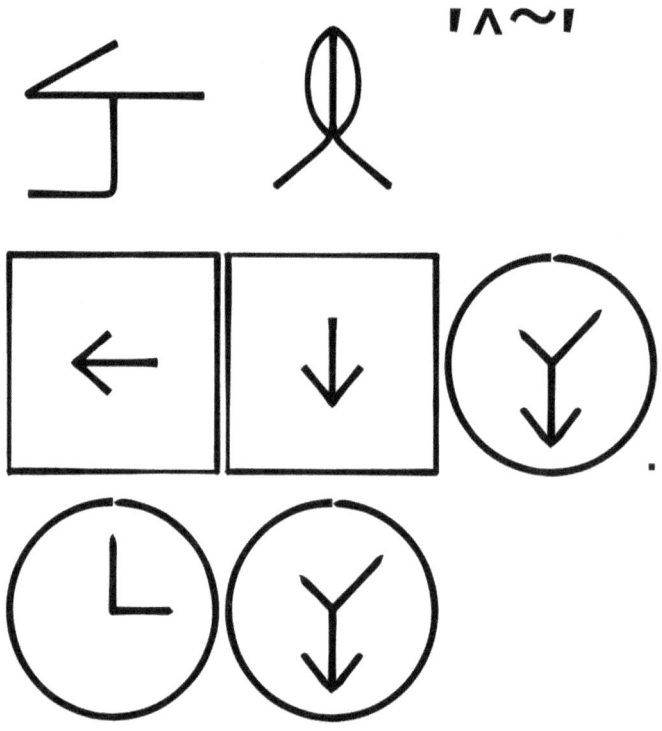

Root Words: (you) (pray)'^~' (left arrow + down arrow = by) (now). (three o'clock) (now).

English Translation: You will have been praying by now. It's three o'clock now.

Grammar Comparison

Simplified Grammar

Simplified grammar emoji:
(}

Simplified grammar kanmoji:
(}

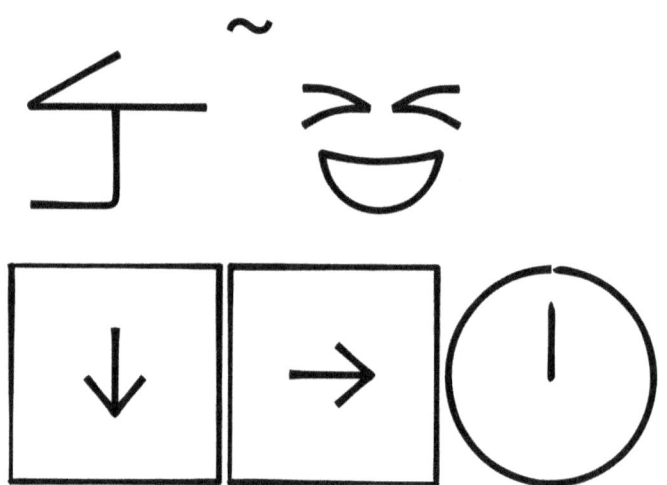

Root Words: (you) ~(laugh) (down arrow + right arrow + twelve o'clock = since twelve o'clock).
English Translation: You are laughing since twelve o'clock.

(This is not accurate, but you get the idea).

In this sentence, the action "laugh" is in stage 3 of a task (doing), therefore we use in progress aspect. An English reader will know that the above sentence means the action "laugh" is still in progress so the translation can be revised to: You have been laughing since twelve o'clock.

(Compatible with present perfect continuous tense in English).

Full Grammar

Full grammar emoji:
(*}

Full grammar kanmoji:
(*}

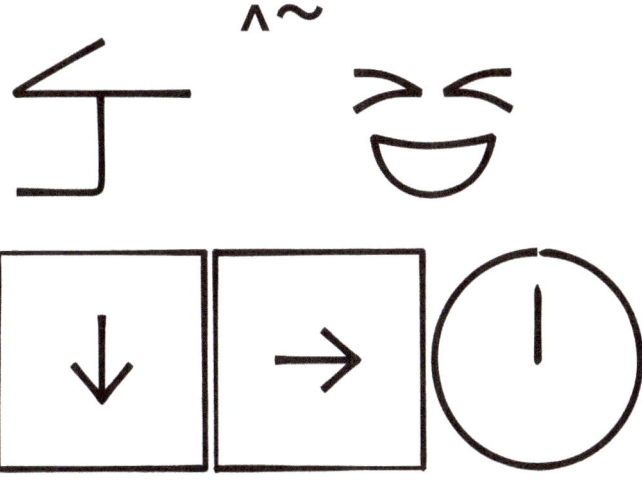

Root Words: (you) ^~(laugh) (down arrow + right arrow + twelve o'clock = since twelve o'clock).

English Translation: You have been laughing since twelve o'clock.

(Compatible with present perfect continuous tense in English).

Acknowledgement

- Emoji images from Twemoji 11.0[1] by Twitter[2] is licensed under CC BY 4.0[3].
- Kanmoji graphics : http://kanmoji.com.
- Emojigraphy hashtags : #Emojigraphy #EmojiLanguage #EmojigraphyLang
- If you like this book, please consider leaving an honest review on your purchase. It will give us the confidence to continue with our projects.
- We will create an adventure novel using Emojigraphy. Go to http://emojigraphy.com/ to subscribe to our updates.

---

1. https://github.com/twitter/twemoji
2. https://github.com/twitter/
3. https://creativecommons.org/licenses/by/4.0/

About the Publisher

Emojigraphy.com has published several books in the series:

- Kanmoji Basic (the first book in the Kanmoji Series)
  http://kanmoji.com
- Emojigraphy The International Emoji Language Basic
  (the first book in the Emojigraphy Series)
  http://emojigraphy.com
- Suumoji Basic (the first book in the Suumoji Series)
  - Upcoming
  http://suumoji.com

Emojigraphy.com has created emoji merchandise:

- T Shirt
  http://emojigraphy.com/merch/

www.ingramcontent.com/pod-product-compliance
Lightning Source LLC
Chambersburg PA
CBHW071220070526
44584CB00019B/3083